Global Cities

MEXICO CITY

Edward Parker
photographs by Edward Parker

Evans

Published by
Evans Brothers Limited,
Part of the Evans Publishing Group,
2A Portman Mansions
Chiltern Street
London WIU 6NR

First published 2006
© copyright Evans Brothers Limited

British Library Cataloguing in Publication Data

Parker, Edward
   Mexico City. - (Global cities)
   1.Mexico City (Mexico) - Juvenile literature
   I.Title
   972.5'30841

ISBN 0 237 53098 8
13-digit ISBN (from 1 January 2007) 9780237 530983

Designer: Robert Walster, Big Blu Design
Maps and graphics by Martin Darlinson

All photos by Edward Parker/IMAGES EVERYTHING LTD. (EASI-Images) except:
Corbis 15, 54, 55t and front cover main image.

Series concept and project management EASI –
Educational Resourcing
(info@easi-er.co.uk)

Contents

Living in an urban world

Sometime in 2007 there will be an estimated 3.3 billion people living in towns and cities. For the first time in history there will be more people living in urban areas than in the countryside.

The urban challenge...

This staggering rate of urbanisation (the process by which a country's population becomes concentrated into towns and cities), is being repeated across much of the world. For example, in China, the world's most populous country, the number of people living in urban areas has already increased from 196 million in 1980 to over 536 million by 2005. Urbanisation presents us with a complex set of challenges for the twenty-first century. Many of these

challenges are local, like the provision of clean water for the growing number of city dwellers. Others are global in scale. Pollution generated by urban areas is one of these global concerns, particularly as urban residents tend to generate more than their rural counterparts. Problems of international crime, including terrorism, are also concentrated in the world's biggest cities. Few cities in the world face problems as severe as those of Mexico City.

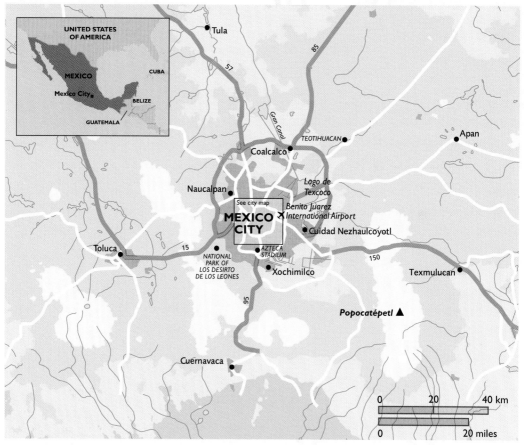

▲ Mexico City, and inset, its relation to the rest of Mexico and neighbouring countries.

... and opportunity

Urban centres, and particularly major cities, also provide great opportunities for improving life at both a local and global scale. Cities concentrate people and allow for efficient forms of mass transport like subway or light rail networks. Services too, such as waste collection, recycling, education and health can all function more efficiently in a city. Cities are also centres of learning and often the birth-place of new ideas, from innovations in science and technology to new ways of day-to-day living. Cities provide a platform for the celebration of arts and culture, too. As the populations of cities become more multi-cultural such cultural celebrations are increasingly global in both their origins and their reach.

▲ An aerial view of the northern part of Mexico City stretching to the mountains.

A global city

Although all urban centres share certain things in common there are a number of cities in which the challenges and opportunities facing an urban world are particularly concentrated. These can be thought of as 'global cities' – cities that in themselves provide a window on the wider world and reflect the important challenges of urbanisation, of globalisation, of citizenship and of sustainable development, that face us all.

Mexico City is one of the world's mega-cities, with a population that is officially over 18 million, but has been estimated to be as high as 24 million. This massive population is continuing to grow. Mexico City has acted as a magnet for people from the rural areas of Mexico for over 100 years – today more people than ever enter the city from outlying states.

The rapid population growth of the city presents major issues for the city authorities. Tens of thousands of new homes, more school places and jobs are needed every year to keep pace with the growing population. However, compared to most parts of Mexico, people living in the centre of Mexico City still have much better access to services such as health care, clean water and electricity.

▲ People gathering in the Zocalo (main square) in Mexico City on Independence Day.

Mexico City is the cultural, economic and industrial centre for the country of Mexico, and represents many of the best and worst features of Mexico. It is the economic powerhouse of the country and the seat of the national government. It is an historic city with elegant colonial buildings, spacious parks and the country's best museums. It has a young population who can enjoy the exciting night life in the centre, watch football at the famous Azteca Stadium or take colourful boat trips on the Aztec canals at Xochimilco. At the same time millions of people in the city live in terrible poverty. The slum settlements at the edges of the city are continually expanding. The

▼ The centre of Mexico City.

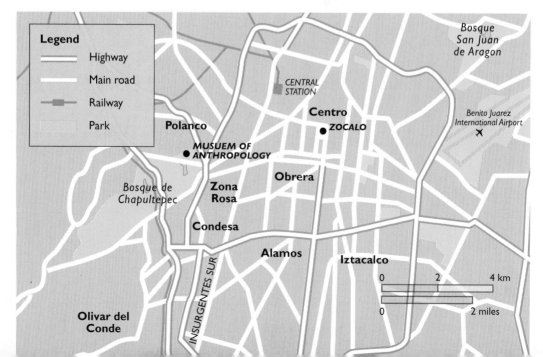

combination of its valley location (Mexico City is situated in the southern part of a mountain valley almost 2,200 m above sea level. It is surrounded by mountains, including active volcanoes, some of which are snow-capped and rise to over 5,000 m), high altitude and its huge numbers of vehicles and factories also means that Mexico City has earned the dubious distinction of being known as 'the world's most polluted city'.

The city is also the second most populous in the world, after Tokyo – its population is similar in size to the entire state of Texas, USA. Fifty years ago Mexico City's population was fewer than three million and the boundaries of the city fell entirely within the Distrito Federal (the Federal District). Because of this Mexicans often refer to their capital as 'El DF'. As the city has grown it has spilled well beyond the boundaries of the Federal District into neighbouring states, in particular the state of (confusingly) Mexico. The city currently covers an area of approximately 2,000 sq km. Because it has expanded beyond its original borders the whole area it now covers is now referred to as the Mexico City Metropolitan Area (MCMA). This includes the Federal District and the new parts of the city that have spread into the surrounding states. In this book, when the term Mexico City is used we will be referring to the MCMA.

The huge divide between rich and poor in the city causes serious social tensions. With so many people migrating to the city the challenges of providing housing and other basic services of water, electricity and health care are immense. Nevertheless, since gaining its own independent mayor and city council in 1997, Mexico City has begun to seriously address its many problems. These include improving the transport system, providing pensions for the elderly, reducing the appalling pollution tackling gun crime, and providing better housing for residents.

▼ People in the wealthy central suburb of Polanco, Mexico City.

The history of Mexico City

The site occupied by Mexico City today has been settled for more than 10,000 years. At the beginning of the period of human habitation, the high valley in which Mexico City is located was mostly occupied by a very large body of water – Lago de Texcoco. The abundant water, temperate climate and fertile volcanic soils provided ideal agricultural conditions for settlers.

Early tribes

By 2000 years ago the population of the valley had grown significantly and the area had become the centre of an empire stretching as far south as Guatemala. The capital of this empire was based at Teotihuacan, located about 25 km to the north of present-day Mexico City. By the seventh century AD the Teotihuacan empire had collapsed and been replaced by a number of distinct city states. The most important was the Toltec empire based at Tula, 65 km north of Mexico City. The Toltec empire had lasted until the thirteenth century, and out of all the different tribes competing for control of the valley, it was the Aztecs who emerged as the most powerful.

▼ A mural by Diego Rivera depicting life in Mexico City during the reign of the Aztecs and before the arrival of the Spanish.

The Aztecs (also called Mexica) were originally a wandering tribe from north-west Mexico that settled on the western shores of Lago de Texcoco. They were a particularly war-like and aggressive tribe, practising human sacrifice and stealing wives from other local tribes. Some time between 1325 and 1345 the Aztecs founded their own city, called Tenochtitlan, on an island on the western shores of Lago de Texcoco. Today the island is part of the area around the main square (Zocalo) in the historic part of down-town Mexico City.

The Aztecs built their city on a grid of canals instead of roads, and developed a unique form of agriculture to make the best of the marshy lake edges where they lived – floating gardens. These floating gardens, called *chinampas*, were made by piling vegetation and mud onto willow branches. These gardens provided three or four harvests a year. However, even these were not enough to feed the growing city population, so the Aztecs conquered other local tribes in order to get agricultural produce, treasures and prisoners to sacrifice. Records show that nearly 20,000 people were sacrificed in 1487 alone.

By 1519 the population of the Aztec city of Tenochtitlan was estimated to be over 200,000, making it one of the largest cities in the world at the time, while the population of the surrounding valley had grown to more than 1.5 million.

▲ Statues excavated from the Aztec pyramid called Templo Mayor in the centre of Mexico City.

▼ Aztec temples were stripped of their stone for later buildings.

The Spanish invasion

From 1519 the previously all-powerful Aztec empire was attacked by a small Spanish army, under the command of Hernan Cortes. Using horses (never before seen by the Aztecs) and guns, they routed the far larger Aztec army and, after a siege lasting 85 days, almost completely destroyed the city of Tenochtitlan.

The valley's population of an estimated 1.5 million collapsed to just 100,000 by 1550. Tens of thousands of Aztecs succumbed to the diseases brought by the Spanish. The Aztec capital was completely rebuilt as the Spanish 'Mexico City', and the country around it became the colony Nueva España, or New Spain.

The reign of Spain

From 1535 New Spain was ruled from Mexico City by a series of viceroys. Large buildings were constructed using volcanic rock from the Aztec pyramids and houses. The large town houses of the new administrators and merchants were built around the central square – the Zocalo. The new Spanish rulers became very rich on the trade of gold and silver from Mexico's mines. By 1800 the population of

Mexico City had risen to 137,000. Spain ruled Mexico from the invasion of Cortes until 1821 – 300 years. In the early part of the nineteenth century Mexicans fought a campaign against Spanish colonial rule. In 1821 a military officer who had joined the independence movement, Agustin de Iturbide, entered Mexico City and made himself emperor. So bad was his rule, though, that the military deposed him within a year. In 1824 Mexico became a republic, and Mexico City was declared the national capital.

Instability

After the end of Spanish rule Mexico suffered terrible instability – 50 governments and 30 presidents attempted to rule the country over the following half century. The French occupied the city from 1863 to 1867, installing the Austrian Archduke Maximilian as an emperor. This political turbulence led to civil chaos, which meant Mexico City was unable to raise money to help fund improvements to its infrastructure.

A military coup led by Porfirio Diaz in 1877 brought this period of instability to an end. Diaz ran the country as a dictatorship. Trade grew and and the city started to

▼ Statue of El Cabillito (the little horse) depicts the Spanish King Charles IV on horseback.

industrialise. While the country was now politically stable, social problems caused by the policies of the Diaz government were causing problems in the working classes – wages declined and the cost of living went up. These social problems led to the Mexican Revolution of 1910.

The Revolution

For ten years after the revolution exploded, Mexico City was rocked by violence. This was a desperate era of hunger and deprivation for the city. Even after the end of the violence conditions did not improve. The city's development was stopped, even though the population

▲ The dashing Pancho Villa (1878-1923) was one of the leaders of the Mexican Revolution, leading peasant armies against the Diaz regime.

began to rise after 1920. Conditions were at their worst in the 1920s and 30s when the population density had risen to a staggering 80,000 people per sq km in some central areas of the city.

After the world-wide Great Depression in the 1930s Mexico City began to industrialise once again and, as a consequence, attracted huge numbers of migrants from rural areas, desperate to escape poverty. By 1940 the city's population stood at 1.7 million. During the 1940s and 1950s Mexico City prospered and skyscrapers started to dot the skyline. New migrants arrived in the city every day, attracted by the booming economy, causing the population of the city to increase by around seven per cent a year. It was impossible for the city authorities to keep pace with the demand for housing and other basic services and, as a consequence, large slums started to develop on the outer edges of the city.

The 1970s and 80s

During the 1970s and 1980s people continued to pour into the city. A huge earthquake in 1985, which killed between 10,000 and 20,000 people, had little effect on the growth of the city, despite widespread destruction. During the 1980s and 1990s Mexico's economy suffered serious and destabilising fluctuations. In 1982 Mexico caused what was known as the Latin American Debt Crisis when it stopped paying the interest on its international loans. These loans had been given by foreign banks and by not paying the interest on what it owed, the country was unable to acquire more money. This resulted in several years of hardship as the economy went into recession. There were further economic problems in the 1990s, but by the new millennium economic conditions had started to improve, as more sustainable economic practices were employed.

The people of Mexico City

The majority of people who live in Mexico City are termed *mestizo* or mixed race. These people are partly descended from Mexican indigenous peoples and Europeans. Some of the city's inhabitants still belong to one of the distinct indigenous Mexican groups and can trace their roots back to the first Mexican people.

In the bustling city it is possible to see the descendants of Aztecs (known as Nahua), Zapotecs from Oaxaca and Mayas from southern Mexico. Other people are descended from the families that arrived during the conquest and the following 300 years of Spanish colonial rule. In addition there are many other people whose ancestors originate from other European, Asian and African countries, some of whom are the descendants of slaves. In recent decades there have also been significant numbers of people migrating to Mexico City who are escaping poverty, war and natural disasters in other Central American countries.

The vast majority of the people who live in Mexico City are Roman Catholics but there are very small numbers of people who are either Protestant or who follow indigenous beliefs.

Growing population

In 1950 Mexico City had fewer than three million inhabitants. In 2006 it is almost seven times larger with some estimates suggesting the figure is over 21 million. During the twentieth century, both the city and structure of the population underwent massive changes. The city attracted migrants from all over Mexico and grew economically as the country continued to industrialise. As the population grew rapidly, the city expanded into new areas increasingly far from its original centre. In half a century the city has expanded 15 times over to cover more than 2,000 sq km, spreading far beyond the original boundaries of the DF into surrounding states. Today nearly a third of the whole country's population lives within 200 km of Mexico City.

The last 20 years has seen the rate of population growth in Mexico City slow down – fewer babies are being born and the proportion of children and adolescents aged 0 to 19 is getting smaller. At the same time the proportion of the population of working age (between 20 and 64) has

◄ Descendants of the Aztecs, known as Nahua.

Manuel Gonzalez, union leader

My name is Jose Manuel Gonzalez and I am a union leader of a small group of people with trades to offer. The union celebrated its 100th anniversary last year and is made up of people offering trades such as electricians, carpenters and plumbers. We can be found at the Zocalo (Mexico City's main square) every day waiting for work. It is hard to get work in the city but, because we are always in the same location, people know where to find us.

I arrived in Mexico City as a child more than 50 years ago. I used to live with my parents in Zacatecas, which is a few hundred kilometres north of the city. One year the rains failed and we were not able to harvest the maize as usual. It meant that our family was starving and eventually my parents moved to Mexico City to look for

work so that they could feed us. Today, my children are at the University studying. I don't want them to be like me and have trouble finding work each day. I want them to get good jobs so they can have some security in their lives.

increased. Because there are so many people of working age the demand for jobs, transport, energy and services such as hospitals is rising.

The average population density of Mexico City today is approximately 12,000 people per sq km. This is very high compared to other megacities around the world. It is slightly higher than that of Tokyo and almost double that of New York, Sao Paulo and Buenos Aires. Only the Asian cities of Mumbai, Calcutta and Hong Kong have higher densities.

▶ Mexico City has a population density of over 12,000 people per square kilometre.

One city, two worlds

Official statistics for Mexico City generally refer to the DF part of the city, which has a population of over nine million. However, this accounts for less than half the whole city's current population. The rest of the city is now mainly in the state of Mexico. This proportion is predicted to rise to 60 per cent by 2010.

The more expensive DF, which includes the areas close to the historical centre, is actually experiencing a fall in population. At the same time more than 10,000 people are arriving every day in the poor areas far from the city centre, making already overcrowded areas even worse.

Where you live in Mexico City makes all the difference to your living conditions. A small percentage of the population is extraordinarily wealthy, and in the main lives close to the centre of the city. More than 20 per cent of the population live below the poverty line and these people tend to live outside the eight *delegaciones* (administrative areas) that make up the city centre.

▼ The wealthy residents of the Zona Rosa in the centre of Mexico City live in air-conditioned homes and drive expensive cars.

Distrito Federal

The DF comprises 16 delegaciones, including the eight that make up the historical centre of the City. These areas experience a very different type of development to those areas on the outer edges.

The DF is the area with the best access to essential services such as hospitals, clean water and sewerage. All of the grand buildings, major universities, national government departments, museums, art galleries, and restaurants are found here.

Generally, the people of European descent enjoy a much higher standard of living than the average, and live in the DF. In contrast, indigenous Mexicans who can trace their ancestry back to the ancient civilisations tend to live in very poor circumstances a long way from the centre of the city.

▲ Women and children in the rubbish-strewn slum of Neahaulcoyotl.

CASE STUDY

Nuria Montiel, DF resident

My name is Nuria Montiel and I live in an apartment in the same block as my parents, in a part of the DF known as Condesa. It is one of the residential suburbs close to the centre of the city and has many colonial buildings and parks.

I am 23, and just finishing a degree in art at UNAM (Mexico City University). Once I have finished I am looking forward to travelling. I have already travelled in Europe, India, USA and Canada but now I would like to see other parts of Latin America.

I was born and brought up in the DF. My family are here and also my friends. It's my home. It has the best entertainment, schools, museums and most of the best jobs are located here. But I fear for the future. Last week we had three days when

we had no water. In the winter months the pollution is so bad that it makes your eyes sting and it's difficult to breathe. The traffic congestion is terrible and violent crime is a major problem. Despite all this I think I will live, or at least base myself in the DF, in the future.

Outlying areas of the city

As Mexico City has expanded it has swallowed whole towns and villages that were once outside the city limits and, in many cases, even in a different state. In 1950 only two municipalities in the bordering state of Mexico were considered to be part of Mexico City. By 2005 40 municipalities that were once part of the state of Mexico were considered to be part of the Mexico City.

The population of these *municipios*, as they are called in Spanish, have grown very rapidly. In 1950 the first two municipalities to become part of Mexico City had a combined population of just 60,000. By 2005 there were over 9.3 million people living in the 40 municipalities. If current trends continue the combined population of the municipalities could reach 12 million by 2010, with people living in much poorer conditions than the inhabitants of the DF.

Mexico City has always acted as a magnet for people in poor areas in other parts of Mexico. However, the cost of land and housing near the centre of the city is too high for people on low wages. As the land is less expensive on the outskirts of the city the poorest people tend to make homes in this area and commute long distances to the jobs in the city centre. Much of the land that is used to build houses on is illegally occupied, including nature reserves or farmland. There are rarely services such as water or electricity.

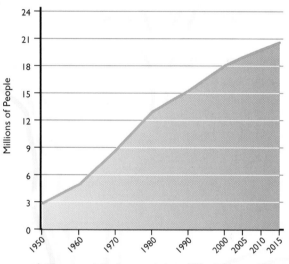

▲ The growth in the population of Mexico over the period 1950 – 2015.

▼ A view from the southern edge of the city. This is where new arrivals to the city build makeshift homes.

▲ The outskirts of Mexico City have swallowed small towns, like Coyocan shown here, not all of which are slums.

Shanty towns

Shanty towns, or slums, are terms used for areas of unplanned urban development. Typically, this is where houses made of the very poorest materials are built on unoccupied land. In Mexico City it is possible to see huge shanty towns built on land that is too steep for regular buildings or on land too close to polluting factories for normal residential areas.

Some of the older shanty towns, such as the enormous Cuidad Nezahaulcoyotl, east of the airport, are huge. Nezahaulcoyotl is home to over three million people. Its residents have secured services such as mains water and electricity. It is not unusual to see the development of better middle class areas in the slum once these services have been provided and as people begin to earn sufficient money to build better homes. Bordering Nezahaulcoyotl is another slum area known as Ixtalapa. This has a population of over 2.5 million people but because it is newer the conditions are even worse.

▼ Teenagers walking on a bridge over a polluted river in the huge slum of Nezahaulcoyotl.

Living in the city

Providing basic services to the population of a city that has experienced such fast, extensive and unplanned growth as Mexico City has proved too difficult for the city's authorities. As new illegal settlements develop government authorities often intervene to try to supply essential urban services like clean water and access to basic education. However, the services can remain inadequate for long periods of time.

Water

Mexico City needs to be able to provide huge quantities of fresh water – between 35,000 and 37,000 litres per second – to be able to keep up with demand. Demand varies between the various city districts. For example, on average the poorest parts of the city use 20 litres a day per person. In the wealthiest parts of the city, such as Polanco and Condesa, the average is 600 litres used by each person per day. By 2010 it is estimated that Mexico City's demand will reach 43,000 litres per second.

Mexico City was once rich in water resources but it now needs to import water long distances into the city. There are three main sources of water for the city. The most important are aquifers (underground water sources) around the city, which currently provide 71 per cent of Mexico City's fresh water. However, the underground water is being over-exploited and more and more water is having to be piped in. Today over a quarter of the city's water comes from the rivers in the states of Mexico and Hidalgo. Many areas have no mains water supply – their water has to be delivered by lorry.

The DF has the best water system in all of Mexico, with 514 km of aqueducts, 910 km of large mains water pipes and a network of 11,900 km of water pipes linking to industry and residential houses.

▼ A water tanker delivering drinking water to a bottling shop in one of the poor slum areas of Mexico City.

Despite all the problems facing Mexico City, 97 per cent of all houses in the DF have access to mains water and over 98 per cent have mains drainage. The situation is very different in the slums away from the centre. Millions have poor access to mains water and mains drainage. These settlements are often located on steeply-sloping land that is a long way from the nearest water main and ill-suited for the laying of pipes. However, city authorities work hard to provide clean water by providing standpipe, mains water and sewerage.

▶ Many people live by earning money by collecting old drinking vessels for recycling that they pull out from their polluted water courses.

CASE STUDY

Lorenzo, Ixtalapa resident

My name is Lorenzo Morales, and I live in Ixtalapa. I have lived alongside the Gran Canal, which carries the "black waters" (sewerage) out of the city, for nearly 20 years. I work as a security guard for a company making machine parts. My house is small, and although the mains water pipes and the Gran Canal both go close to my house, I still don't have mains water or sewerage. It means that I have to buy water each week from trucks that visit the area. I store it on the roof in a tank and try to use as little as possible. The Gran Canal often stinks, especially when the water is low. People say it is unhealthy to live near it but I haven't been ill yet. Even though it smells I don't want to move. I have been here a long time and it's my land now. Also I know most of the people around me and we all help each other as best we can.

Energy

The rapidly growing population and industry of Mexico City has created a major demand for energy. Currently around 87 per cent of all energy demands in the city are met by fossil fuels. Fossil fuels are typically petrol, diesel and liquid petroleum gas (LPG) for vehicles. For industry the main fuels used are diesel and industrial gas oil. The remaining 13 per cent of the demand is met by electricity generated outside the city.

The provision of mains electricity follows much the same pattern as water services. Close to 100 per cent of homes within the central DF have access to mains electricity. The parts of the city outside the DF area, which include the many slums, have poor access to electricity. Cooking

▲ Many residents of the shanty towns steal energy by tapping into the mains electricity supplies.

▲ A truck delivering gas to one of the slums which does not have the full range of basic services.

24

and heating is carried out using portable sources of energy – gas in cylinders or what wood can be collected from the surrounding environment.

Housing

There is high demand for new houses in Mexico City. In the central DF area the houses being constructed are for the middle classes and the wealthy.

Beyond the DF the housing is often very basic with large families living in small, makeshift single storey houses. As the settlements are often illegal, there is little incentive for residents to build houses out of good materials because of the fear of being moved on by the city authorities and their homes then being torn down.

The city and national governments have huge housing programmes constructing tens of thousands of 'affordable' houses every year. However, it is extremely difficult to keep pace with the new arrivals, and these newly-built homes quickly become desirable, and so more expensive.

CASE STUDY

Maria Mohuel, Ixtalapa resident

I moved to Ixtalapa more than 30 years ago when the area was mainly fields. Ixtalapa was right on the edge of the city when I arrived and it's still a very poor area. However, after spending many years carrying water to the house we now have access to mains water. The gas cylinders we use are still delivered by truck. This year I applied for a loan from the government to improve my house. I have three sons and four grandchildren and I wanted them to be able to live here if they need to. I was given an interest-free loan of US$400 (which I have to pay back over five years) to build a second storey on our small house and improve the bathroom. Without this loan it would have been impossible for me to improve my house.

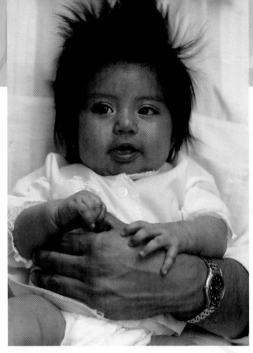

▲ Small children are particularly at risk of developing respiratory diseases caused by air pollution.

Health

Providing health care in Mexico City is another huge challenge. The city is a very unhealthy place to live and, with more than four million people living below the poverty line, many residents cannot afford even the most basic medical care. Mexico City has a serious problem with air pollution, which creates a high number of respiratory illnesses, such as bronchitis and lung cancer. The pollution also seriously affects other groups such as asthma sufferers.

Poor drainage and waste management has led to outbreaks of cholera and typhoid in the city. Despite this, the city, and especially the DF, has the best health care system in the country. The city is home to most of the main teaching hospitals in Mexico.

Education

Mexico City has both the best and worst examples of education in the country. It is home to the largest and oldest university in north and south America – UNAM. Established in 1550, it has more than 300,000 students and 40,000 teachers. Mexico City also has many of the best

primary and secondary schools in Mexico. However, these are almost exclusively located in DF.

In the outlying areas access to education is very variable. People who live on the fringes have access to only the most basic education services and children are often required to work from an early age to help the income of the family. The city authorities try to provide basic education in the poorest areas of the city and there are even schools located on or close to the huge city waste dumps for the children of people who make a living picking through the rubbish.

As well as providing schools there are other great educational problems for the city authorities to overcome. In 2005 all 58,000 primary and secondary school teachers in Mexico City went on strike to protest against cuts in pay and cuts in expenditure on school materials proposed by the national governments.

▼ Getting a good education depends on where you live. These children are at school in the DF.

Donjaji Lopez, teacher

My name is Donjaji Lopez and I am a teacher working with both primary and secondary students. I enjoy working with children and I really like this job because I have the chance to teach children of different ages and from both private and public schools about the environment of Mexico City.

I used to work in a primary school. The pay was very poor and we had very little money to spend on materials. The children were eager to learn and many of the parents were very happy for their children to be at school as it was an opportunity that they did not have themselves when they were younger.

There is a great demand on school places in Mexico City and in many schools there is a double shift operating. One group of children have their school day from 7 am to 12 noon and another group from 1 pm until 6 pm. In this way double the number of students can use the same numbers of schools.

▶▼ Donjaji working with a class.

The Mexico City economy

Mexico City is one of Latin America's prime commercial cities – second only in economic muscle to Sao Paulo in Brazil. Mexico City is the heart of the nation's financial sector and a major location for industry. The economy is based on trade, finance, insurance, textiles, making automotive parts, agricultural processing, construction, mining, engineering, and biotechnology. The entire federal government is based in Mexico City, as are the Mexican stock exchange and many of the country's banks, insurers and most of the multinational firms based in Mexico.

The country's economic power house

Mexico City contributes 33 per cent of Mexico's national economy – which was worth just over US$1 trillion in 2004. The city's economy has grown faster than the national average since 1980. A severe national economic slump in the mid 1990s was the worst for 50 years (caused by devaluing the currency), but the national economy has recovered and is growing at 6.9 per cent per year.

The economy of Mexico City, like the whole country, is dependent on the stability of the nation's currency, the peso. In times when the Mexican currency is unstable the economy suffers. Also, Mexico has huge debts that affect the prosperity of the

▼ A large cement factory in the northern, industrial zone of Mexico City.

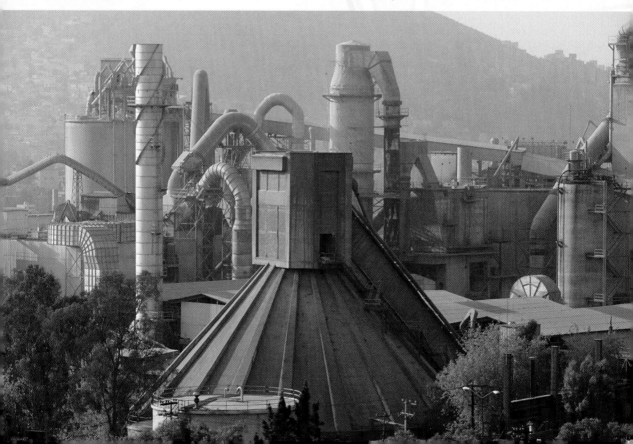

▲ Cars manufactured in Mexico City.

▲ Headquarters of the Mexican stock market.

country. In 1982 Mexico caused what was known as the Latin American Debt Crisis. This was when Mexico refused to pay the interest on its loans from wealthier countries. The result was that loans for building roads, dams and factories, for example, were stopped and Mexico was forced to alter its economy to be able to pay back the money. Not only did the wealth of Mexicans sharply decline, but the manufacturing industries turned their attention to the more lucrative business of producing goods for export to help to pay the interest on loans. The payment of the interest on Mexico's vast loans is still the country's single largest payment every year. In the last few years it has varied between US$12 and 13.5 billion a year. With a rapidly growing economy the city government has

more opportunity to spend money on Mexico City's infrastructure, such as roads and telecommunications.

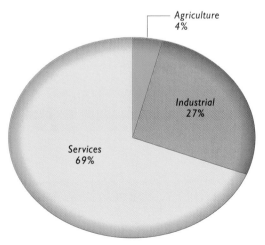

Agriculture 4%

Industrial 27%

Services 69%

▲ The structure of the city economy in terms of GDP contributions or employment contribution.

▲ Open-cast mining takes place within the city limits. Most mining is for material for the construction industry.

Manufacturing

Most of Mexico City's manufacturing industry is based on chemicals, plastics, cement and textiles. Construction is another important aspect of the city economy – as the economy has started to improve more and more modern buildings are being built. There are even a few small mines within the city limits. Manufacturing and construction account for 23 per cent of the city economy, but that figure is dropping. Some of the manufacturing processes used are out-of-date and inefficient.

Services

The industries of the service sector include banking, insurance, computer programming and tourism. In addition the service sector includes public services provided by the government such as hospitals, mains water and electricity.

In the last 50 years Mexico has transformed itself from primarily an agricultural and mining economy into a modern industrialised economy characterised by a large service sector. In Mexico City it is estimated that 75 per cent of the economy is provided by the service sector. In contrast agriculture and manufacturing are declining in importance.

The service industry is the most important part of the whole Mexican economy in terms of employment, and this is particularly true in Mexico City. This growth in the service sector has been very important for women, as there are typically more jobs available to women in the service sector than in other parts of the economy. So, with a growing service sector has come large increases in the numbers of women working in Mexico City.

Jose Lopez, waiter

My name is Jose Alonso Lopez. I have worked for many years as a waiter in a hotel in the centre of the city. Every morning I leave my house at 5.15 am to make sure I am at work in time to start serving the breakfasts at 7 am. This is because I live in Nezahualcoyotl, and it is a long way outside the city centre. I take a *pesero* (micro bus) to the end of the Metro line and come in the rest of the way by Metro. It's very crowded but only costs 2 pesos (about 20 US cents).

I am lucky to have a job but I work from 7 am until 3 pm for just 42 pesos (US$4) a day. I hope to make more money with tips but I still find it hard to earn enough money to support my family.

Agriculture

Surprisingly, there are still areas in the south of the central DF where there are large areas of agricultural land. In the area of Xochimilco, for example, people continue to use the Aztec-style *chinampas* (floating gardens) to produce thousands of tonnes of fresh vegetables and cut flowers. Other, higher, areas are used to grow maize, nogales (edible cacti) and for the raising of cattle and other animals.

▼ These small rectangular floating gardens of vegetables can produce several harvests a year.

The informal economy

The informal economy is where people work in jobs which are not officially registered. They are generally paid in cash and because of this do not pay tax to the government. The advantage to the employer is that they can offer low wages and do not have any of the legal responsibilities for the workers, such as when someone is injured at work.

There are many types of work in the informal economy, including newspaper sellers, waiters, and market traders. Unemployment is a major problem in Mexico City, especially for people over 35 years old. Many people have to do whatever they can to earn a few pesos a day in order to eat. There are so many people desperate for work that people offering jobs can afford to pay very low wages, sometimes even below the minimum salary of 42 pesos or US$4 a day.

▲ A woman making bracelets to sell on her market stall.

CASE STUDY

Aturo Gomez, newspaper seller

My name is Aturo Gomez and I work every morning on the Paseo de la Reforma selling newspapers to drivers who stop at the traffic lights. I like to work from 7 am until 1 pm and then go home to continue my studies. I am a student and I need the money to pay my college fees. I am studying computer programming at UNAM, and when I have qualified I am hoping to get a job in one of the big offices round here.

Selling newspapers earns me enough money to survive. I don't have to pay tax and, as a student, I have some benefits in terms of health care.

I quite like the job because I am young and have no responsibilities. A group of us work the same piece of road every day and most of us are studying. We are studying hard because it must be terrible to have to support a family with work like this.

In 2000 the government department of the National Institute of Statistics, Geography and Informatics (INEGI) carried out a survey to measure the size of Mexico's informal economy. The figures revealed that excluding illegal activities such as drug trafficking, the informal sector had a value of US$47 billion. However, some other studies have put the size of the informal economy in Mexico at around US$150 billion a year.

Mexico City is one of the largest single labour markets in the world, with over seven million economically active people. About 40 per cent of those working in the city were classified as being in the informal sector. Most of these people work in shops and restaurants or sell products and services by the city's roads. These enterprises are typically small-scale. Wages are low and the people involved are not usually covered by social security or other forms of public welfare protection.

The city government is trying to address the problem of the informal sector through

▲ Shoe shining is one way to make money.

a range of well-meaning initiatives, but widespread corruption and the resistance of those employers that benefit from the situation mean that little of significance has been achieved, despite the financial benefits to the city that taxes on informal sector workers would bring.

▼ There are millions of underemployed and unemployed people in Mexico City. Many advertise their services by putting signs in the street.

Managing Mexico City

Managing a city the size of Mexico City is a daunting challenge. Until 1997 the national government, based in the centre of the city, made the main decisions about the running of the DF. Fifty years ago the whole of Mexico City fell within the DF, but today, with around half of the urban area of the city outside the DF, the rest of the city is in the state of Mexico, a much poorer administration than the DF, with fewer financial resources for dealing with the problems of such a large urban area.

Local authorities

The state of Mexico not only has to provide services for the 10 million people who live in the urban area of Mexico City, but also all the other people in a very large state. This causes a sharp divide between the parts of the city that are within the DF and those in the state of Mexico. In order to help manage the city in the twenty-first century the national government has begun to let more decisions about running the city be taken at a local level. In 1997 a mayor of Mexico City was elected for the first time. They were given control of the city budget, and political leaders were elected to posts to manage the city's services, such as transport, water, health and housing. These changes have made it easier to manage the city. Changes have been slow to come, but it is hoped that the city will become more integrated and services will be provided to those areas that need them most.

▼ Anti-corruption protesters campaigning in the street.

▲ Historic buildings such as the Bellas Artes Theatre need expensive maintenance by the city authorities because of subsidence and earthquake damage.

CASE STUDY

Luis Marquez Morales, council employee

My name is Luis Marquez Morales. I work in the Alamada Park clearing the garbage for Cuauhtemoc council. It is one of the finest parks in Mexico City and I work hard to make sure that it is always clean. I have worked here for the last 26 years. I started when I was 35 and I am now 61. I earn 120 pesos ($12 a day) but the cost of living is high in the centre of town and the money does not go very far.

I have worked for Cuauhtemoc council for a long time and I have been in Mexico during the economic problems of the 1980s and 1990s when life was terrible in the city. Since 2000 things have really begun to change. The city centre is being cleaned up. There are new hotels being built where the ones damaged by the earthquake (1985) used to be.

There is also a new trolley bus route being built along Insurgentes Avenue. It feels like things are getting better and that someone cares about the city.

The mayor's problems

In 1997 Andres Manuel Lopez Obrador became Mexico City's first elected mayor. He was elected for a six-year term and began many programmes to try to improve the city. The mayor was given increased powers to try to address the many problems affecting not only the Federal District but also the areas of the city that fall in the state of Mexico. The first of his many programmes was the setting up of social assistance allowances for the elderly, single mothers and the handicapped. He has set up schemes working with teenagers in areas of high crime in order to help them attend school and colleges, and he has begun work on building a new university in the city and his school building programme has created 9,000 new school places.

One of the many problems facing the people of Mexico City is the need for affordable housing near their places of work. The mayor is currently changing legislation so that affordable housing can be built closer to the centre of the city. This would help many people because the

▲ The second level of freeway over the western part of the city under construction.

poorest paid workers typically live in the slums that ring the city and often spend several hours a day on buses and trains going to and from work.

One of the new mayor's most successful achievements is the building of a second level of freeway over the western part of the city, in order to help with traffic congestion. He has also been responsible for renovating Chapultepec Park, which covers four sq km in the heart of the city.

Despite the elected mayors and their increased powers the problems of managing the city are still formidable. There is also tension between the national president and the mayor – in 2005 the national government cut the wages of teachers in the city, which led to strikes in UNAM and in schools and colleges.

A sinking city

The politicians that govern Mexico City are now trying to improve the City as best they can. However, the problems are so enormous that it will cost hundreds of millions of dollars to implement the

◄ The elderly, single mothers and the handicapped have benefited from the mayor's social assistance allowances.

programmes to provide fresh water, improve transport, reduce crime and improve air quality. One of the greatest problems facing the city is beneath it. The city is situated on an old, drained lake bed. The lake bed is still unstable and the whole city has sunk due to the over-extraction of groundwater to meet the city's needs. In the last 100 years the centre of the city has dropped by nine metres, leaving drains exposed, cracking roads, pavements and buildings. This creates an enormous expense for the city, as repairs are continually having to be made. Mexico City is also located on a tectonic fault line and suffers from major earthquakes every few hundred years. In addition there are live volcanoes close to the city, which may erupt at any point. These phenomena make Mexico City even more difficult to manage than it would be otherwise.

CASE STUDY

Enrique Lomeli

My name is Enrique Lomeli and I work in the tallest building in Mexico City, the Torre Mayor. The building is 55 storeys or 225m tall, and has a helipad on the roof. It currently has around 6,000 people working in it. The building is right in the heart of the city's financial district and the

offices here are mainly filled by banks and insurance companies.

Mexico City is very vulnerable to earthquakes and in 1985 more than 10,000 people died in the largest one in recent years. This is because most of the city is built on an old lake bed, which has the effect of amplifying the tremors of an earthquake. The Torre Mayor is a special building because it is designed to withstand major earthquakes. The building is very strong but it also has huge pistons around the foundations that act like shock absorbers. These are filled with silica gel and are designed to absorb the tremors of an earthquake.

◀ Looking up at the Torre Mayor

Transport for Mexico City

In Aztec times the streets of what is Mexico City were canals and the main form of transport was by boat. Today, Mexico City is the transport hub of the entire country, with connections to the rest of the country by road, rail and air. The good links to Mexico City have encouraged millions of people to migrate to the city over the last 50 years. There are over four million private cars on the poorly planned and maintained streets of the city.

▲ Cars, buses and the Metro system (on the left of the picture) all heading into the centre of the city.

Transport systems

As the city has grown the different types of transport systems have developed at different rates. These include private car, taxis, buses, micro-buses (or *pesero*), metro trains, bicycles and national and international air travel. The trend over the last 20 years is for people to choose smaller vehicles to meet their transport needs. This means that the numbers of private cars, taxis and micro-buses has increased massively.

The Metro

Opened the year after the 1968 Mexico City Olympics, the Metro is the quickest way to get around Mexico City. However, it is also the most crowded, carrying around 4.3 million people on a typical weekday. This makes it the third-busiest underground railway in the world after Tokyo and Moscow.

There are more than 170 stations and over 200 km (planned to be 400 km by 2020) of track. The Metro is continually growing to try to meet the demands of the city's growing population. New stations are being constructed, but almost all the stations fall within the eight central *delegaciones* of the DF, and all the Metro lines end at the boundary between the DF and the state of Mexico. Rush hours, which are between 7.30 and 10 in the morning and 5 and 7 in the evening, are frighteningly crowded. Outside the rush hour the

▲ The Metro being used during off-peak hours. Many of the city's workers commute long distances to reach the metro, and then have another long journey into work by train.

service is much easier to use. The cost is low with any single journey of any distance costing 2 pesos (US$0.20).

The Metro is the most efficient public transport system in the city both in terms of the numbers of passengers carried and in terms of energy. Despite being the fastest and least polluting of all the transport options in Mexico City people would rather use a private car if given the chance. As the city's economy develops people have better access to private cars and other forms of travel. Also, the Metro has developed a reputation for being dangerous to travel on, because of a high number of muggings and attacks on passengers.

As the city expands many people find that other types of transport such as micro-buses offer more flexibility.

▼ A micro-bus, or pesero, stuck in rush-hour traffic. These buses are a popular form of transport.

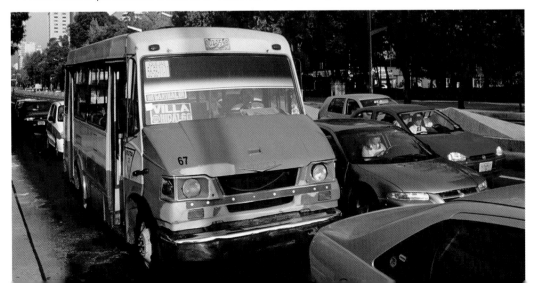

▲ Trolley buses are quieter and and less polluting than other forms of transport.

Buses

Mexico City has a highly developed network of bus services. As the city is the hub of all national bus travel it has four large bus terminals positioned at the four compass points of the city, to cope with the large volumes of passengers that arrive in and depart the city each day. Buses from these terminals also connect with other

CASE STUDY

Pedro Gonzalez, *pesero* driver

I am a *pesero* (micro-bus) driver in Coyocan. Since I have been driving *pesero* there seem to be more and more vehicles on the roads every day. In rush hour it can take an hour to travel just a few kilometres. By 10 am everything has calmed down again, and I can drive my route in very little time. By 1.30 pm the traffic has built up once again as people collect their children from school and people go home for lunch. There is another quiet time in the middle of the afternoon but it all builds up again until between 6 and 9 pm

everywhere is totally crowded. I like seeing the same people each day and generally there is very little trouble on the bus. Coyocan is a pretty and peaceful part of the city so I am quite lucky really.

parts of the city. Around 2.5 million people use the buses and micro-buses daily and the current trend is for the smaller micro-buses to replace the larger buses. Millions of poor people rely on buses to commute from the areas of poor housing on the outlying parts of the city to their places of work in the city centre or other parts of the DF.

Private cars and taxis

During the last 20 years the construction of new highways has struggled to keep up with the massive population expansion in Mexico City and the demand for transport. The use of taxis and private cars is going to increase. The number of taxis is expected to rise above the 110,000 that drive the streets of the capital today.

▼ Private car use continues to rise.

Air travel

Benito Juarez International airport in Mexico City is one of the busiest in Latin America, with 18 million people passing through every year. As well as being a major international airport it is also the hub of Mexico's extensive internal flight network. To ease the burden on the airport the government is considering building a second airport at Texcoco. The current airport is located very close to the centre of Mexico City, and the road congestion caused by passengers coming to the airport is growing year on year. The government is hoping to alleviate some of that congestion by siting the second airport further from the centre of the city. This will also help to reduce the impact of the pollution caused by the aeroplanes in the city centre.

▼ A flight arriving at Mexico City airport.

Culture, leisure and tourism

There is a vast choice of entertainment in Mexico City. There are many cultural activities such as visiting museums, viewing one of the many art exhibitions or spending an evening at the famous Bellas Artes theatre. In addition Mexicans love a fiesta (party) and in the city there are a wide range of venues to see live music. Like all cities of global importance it is possible to see everything from a classical orchestra to one of the world's most famous pop bands any night of the week.

In the Federal District there are 77 museums, 385 cinemas, three zoos, seven football stadiums, four bullrings, as well as one of the finest theatres in Latin America – the Teatro de Bellas Artes.

Mexico City is the centre of almost everything in Mexico. It has the best museums and a number of these a located around the central Chapultepec Park. The Anthropology Museum is globally famous, with world-class exhibits on the culture of Mexico including artefacts from the Aztecs, Mayas and Toltecs. Close by is the Museum of Modern Art. There are many locations in the city where it is possible to see the art

▲ The Teatro de Bellas Artes was built in the early part of the twentieth century. It seats 3,500 people for performances of opera and theatre.

▼ The Anthropology Museum contains important collections of Mayan, Toltec and Aztec artefacts.

of Mexico. Murals of the famous artist Diego Rivera line the interior walls of presidential palace and show images from Mexico's troubled history (see p. 12).

Family recreation

The family remains the focal point of most Mexicans' lives, and the most popular holidays of the year are enjoyed together. Birthdays and weddings are important, as are Semana Santa (Easter), Independence Day (September 16), Dia de Nuestra Senora Guadelupe (December 12 – when the Virgin Mary apparently appeared in a northern suburb of Mexico City in 1531), All Saints Day (November 1) and the Day of the Dead (November 2). For weddings and family parties it is traditional to hire a *mariachi* band. These bands can be seen dressed like characters from the Mexican Revolution, lining the Plaza Garibaldi waiting to play popular Mexican songs for those that will pay them. There are also many salsa and samba clubs where families

▲ On Independence Day children dress up like famous Mexican bandits and revolutionaries.

go to enjoy Latin music. Families often meet at the weekend to visit a park, to go shopping or have a family outing to the pyramids of Teotihuacan or to see the volcanoes outside the city.

▼ A *mariachi* band playing traditional songs. Such bands are a familiar sight in Mexico City.

▲ Sports, like this game of basketball, are common in the residential areas of the city.

Open spaces

Mexico City has many attractions for those who have money and time on their hands. It has many large inner city parks where people can enjoy a leisurely walk or participate in many types of sports. The most popular Sunday amateur sport is football but it is possible to see many games of basketball, tennis and volleyball.

Downtown is one of the largest and oldest of all of Mexico City's parks. It is called Bosque de Chapultepec, or Chapultepec Park. Chapultepec is a Nahua (Aztec language) word meaning hill of the grasshoppers. It was a park before the Spanish arrived and was the location of the Aztec rulers' summer palace and the first zoo in the Americas. Today the zoo has been expanded and the park, which covers four sq km, has hundreds of swamp cypress trees, which were sacred to the Aztecs. Under Spanish rule a castle was built in the park. Thousands of people wind their way up the path to the castle on the hill to enjoy the views over the city. There are also many parks in the prosperous suburbs of the city.

▼ Chapultepec Park is a popular destination with tourists and locals alike.

▲ Tourists on the canals of Xochimilco.

One of the most popular green areas for city dwellers is Xochimilco. Situated about 20 km south of the historic centre, Xochimilco has been absorbed in the spreading city. Nevertheless, it has large areas of wetlands and ancient Aztec canals. Along with the chance to see wildlife in this ecological reserve many people enjoy a trip on one of the colourful boats along the quiet canals.

The famous volcano Popocatepetl is 70 km south-east of the city centre. It is the second highest volcano in North America, and is permanently capped with snow and ice. Its name is a Nahua word meaning 'smoking mountain'. It last erupted in 1994, and has been closed to climbing and hiking since, but nearby mountains are still a very popular destination.

▶ Hikers in the mountains to the south of Mexico City.

▲ The Azteca Stadium has hosted two football World Cup Finals – in 1970 and 1986.

Spectator sports

The young population of Mexico City love their sport. Not only do they take the chance to play in the many parks but they also like to attend football matches, volleyball games and bullfights. Mexico City has some of the largest stadiums in the world. For football there is the Azteca Stadium, home to the Division One team, America, which can hold more than 100,000 fans. The Olympic stadium at UNAM holds 80,000, and, when important football matches are held, the atmosphere inside the bowl is said to be like being in the core of a volcano.

Mexico City has one baseball team in the national baseball league, called the Red Devils (Diablos Rojos). They play in front of sell out crowds three times a week during the season that runs between March and August. Like many former colonies of Spain there is a large following for bullfighting. On weekends between October and March spectators flock to bullfights in the monumental Plaza Mexico – a massive concrete arena than can hold up to 48,000 people.

The value of tourism

Tourism is one of the most valuable service industries because it generates foreign income. Nationally it employs over two million people, 400,000 of whom work in Mexico City. Mexico is one of the most popular holiday destinations in the world, with over 10 million people visiting annually. Around a fifth of those who arrive enter the country through Mexico City.

Mexico City has a well-developed tourist infrastructure, with over 600 hotels and other places for people to stay. Altogether these offer over 46,000 beds. In 2003 there were 10,438,037 visitors to the city, of whom more than six million stayed in the historic centre of the city, the area known as Cuauhtemoc.

Mexico City has a particularly strong history of modern art and it is possible to see many important works in the Museum of Modern Arts. In 2003 the city's museums registered more than 3.6 million visitors in the same year – 10 per cent were international tourists and the rest Mexican nationals. The city and the surrounding area have a rich archeological heritage. In the city centre there is the Aztec pyramid of the Templo Mayor (see page 13). Twenty five kilometres north of the city centre is Teotihuacan, one of the largest pyramid complexes in the world, and built by an unknown people. The city's archeological sites received around 360,000 visitors in 2003, and around 30,000 were foreigners.

The tourists visiting the city also come to see some of the finest Spanish colonial buildings in the Americas. For many it is also a place of Catholic pilgrimage with tens of thousands of people visiting the Basilica de Guadelupe to see the shrine of the Virgin de Guadelupe. The shrine has been associated with a number of apparent miracles.

▼ Part of the pyramid complex of Teotihuacan. The giant pyramids were started in the first century A.D.

The Mexico City environment

Mexico City is located in a high valley known as the Basin of Mexico. It is an area surrounded by mountains on all sides with a wide variety of different environments, from swamps and deserts to cool pine and oak forests. However, over the last 50 years Mexico City has expanded to cover more than 2,000 sq km. This has drastically reduced the wetlands and forest habitats that dominated the area.

Urbanisation

The major urbanisation of the area around the centre of Mexico City has given rise to many other environmental problems other than habitat loss. Such a massive city needs very large amounts of water to supply its daily needs, and with much of the water being taken from the aquifer beneath the city, the old lake bed the city is built on is sinking. The centre of the city has dropped nine metres in 100 years. With such a huge population Mexico City also creates huge quantities of waste, the disposal of which is a major and unsolved problem. Industry and the city's huge population have caused serious pollution of the few rivers that flow through the area.

Habitats and wildlife

The valley of Mexico and Mexico City are two of the areas in the country most intensively studied by zoologists. Studies have found a very high number of species within the city limits – a remarkable

▼ The Angel of Independence, the stone column below, has had 23 steps added so its base can be reached. The city has sunk around it.

▲ Egrets on one of the lakes of the Xochimilco Ecological Reserve, inside the boundaries of the Federal District.

concentration for such a large city.
For example, research undertaken by UNAM revealed that there are 84 species of mammals, 113 species of birds, 59 species of reptiles, 23 species of amphibians and 15 species of fish found inside the DF alone. Of these 23 species are endemic, which means that they are found only in the DF or the valley of Mexico and nowhere else.

The expanding city, however, is putting a number of species at risk of extinction. The populations of most species have declined rapidly over the last 50 years,

and two species of mammals, six species of birds, one species of reptile, and two species of amphibians are believed to be in imminent danger of extinction.

Within the very centre of the city there are a number of large parks, such as Chapultepec Park (see p. 44), the Viveros of Coyocan and the grounds of UNAM. These green areas provide essential, but threatened habitats to some of Mexico's rarest species, including a variety of native rabbits and even white-tailed deer.

Waste management

The removal of rubbish and other waste materials is one of the biggest challenges facing Mexico City. Not only is the population rapidly expanding, but the economy is growing too. It is estimated that the economy of the city will continue to grow by around five per cent per year for the next decade. This fast growth will improve the incomes of millions of people in the city, who in turn will consume more and produce more waste. Currently 19,850 tonnes of waste is piled into the city's landfill sites every day. Around 8,000 workers are employed to collect and dispose of the waste. Each truck carries on average 20 to 25 tonnes of garbage which means that every day around 1,000 truck journeys are required to keep pace with the mounting pressure for waste disposal.

The sources of garbage can be broken down into three main areas – domestic waste, industrial waste and waste from public services such as hospitals. While domestic rubbish accounts for the largest volume of waste, industry is the largest producer of dangerous waste such as poisonous chemicals.

The landfill sites for disposing of waste are sited in the poorest areas of the city, such as Nezahualcoyotl. However, the sheer volume of waste produced every day means that new sites have been opened up outside the Federal District in the state of Mexico. Thousands of people live and work on the garbage dumps. The owners of the businesses that employ the workers that sift through the rubbish are often very wealthy. This is because there are large quantities of materials that can be recycled in the waste that can be sold.

The waste arriving at the landfill sites can be divided into three main types – organic waste such as fruit and vegetable peelings, recyclable materials such as paper, glass and metals, and other waste such as aerosol cartons and construction waste.

▼ Much of the waste produced in the outlying areas beyond the borders of the DF is dumped locally, with much of it finding its way into the local water courses. The water may already be polluted with industrial chemicals.

Water pollution

Mexico City also has many problems with water pollution. Because of the unusual geology of the area there are few rivers, but large underground aquifers. Those rivers and canals that do run through Mexico City are extremely polluted. The three main sources of pollution are industrial, domestic and agricultural. The industrial effluent is the most toxic but domestic sewage is by far the largest in terms of quantity. Most of the waste water from Mexico City heads out of the city in huge tubes or open sewers. Nearly 100 km north of the city the contaminated water is used to irrigate farmland over an enormous area. This farmland acts as a gigantic treatment plant and the springs that flow to the north of this area produce water fit to drink. This is the safest means of processing sewerage away from the city population. Similar methods of dealing with polluted water are used in other cities.

CASE STUDY

Carlos Munoz, economist

My name is Carlos Munoz and I work at the National Institute of Economics. I am an economist and I have the job of studying how money is spent in Mexico City, and if there are ways of making savings. My personal interest is in water provision. I believe that if more people had better access to clean water and sewerage then the city would benefit by millions of dollars. I am studying the health costs associated with people being ill from drinking unclean water and getting infections from untreated sewerage. Thousands of people are ill every year because of poor water costing the health service millions of dollars. Also, tens of thousands of working days are lost each year because people have to take time off work because of illnesses carried in untreated water. The calculation I am making is, how much will it cost to provide better water and how much would the city save in the long run? Each part of the city's services are being evaluated like this and the job of running the city should become easier because the whole urban area is now the responsibility of one authority (see p. 34).

Air pollution

Mexico City has the reputation of being one of the most polluted cities in the world. Every year more than four million tonnes of pollutants are released into the atmosphere from the metropolitan area of Mexico City. There are a number of reasons why air pollution is particularly bad in the city. Apart from its huge numbers of people, vehicles and industries, Mexico City is situated at an altitude of 2,200 m, and surrounded on all sides by mountains, making the already bad situation worse.

During the winter the cold air creates what is known as a temperature inversion. This is where layers of cold air above the city prevent the air pollution from dispersing. This situation can last for many days, and is when the air quality is at its worst in the city. People can suffer from breathing difficulties and skin disorders.

Another problem of the altitude is that the sun is stronger than it would be at sea-level. The strong sunlight causes the mixture of chemicals in the air to react with one another, producing a particularly toxic gas called ozone.

There are many types of air pollution produced from a variety of different sources. The pollutants include toxic gases such as sulphur dioxide, carbon monoxide and ozone. Carbon monoxide is the single largest polluting gas, accounting for 58.8 per cent of all air pollution. There is another group of pollutants which is even more serious in terms of health problems. These are 'suspended particles' – tiny particles produced by diesel engines and dust from soil erosion. This is the part of the air pollution that is visible as the brown smog that often covers the city. These

▼ Smog clouds over the city centre. The strong sunlight at altitude makes the pollution worse.

▲ The mountains prevent air pollution from dispersing quickly, increasing the health problems for the city.

particles have been shown to be a very serious health risk. One recent study calculated that the cost of illnesses, death and days off work cost Mexico City more than US$1 billion dollars a year.

The most significant source of air pollution is transport. Around 75 per cent of all the air pollution produced in Mexico City every year is caused by its buses, trucks and cars. Power stations cause 10 per cent of the air pollution while air pollution produced by industry accounts for just three per cent. Today there are around four million vehicles making an estimated 30 million journeys every day and consuming 16.2 million litres of fuel. The numbers of vehicles in Mexico City is set to double in the next 20 years.

▶ The rate of vehicle use shows no signs of slowing, despite the pollution caused by so many cars on the roads.

Positive initiatives

There are many positive initiatives that have been undertaken to improve the quality of the environment in Mexico City. These range from setting up protected areas as refuges for rare wildlife, to schemes to reduce the pollution from vehicles.

Around Mexico City there is a network of protected areas. These include the National Park of Los Desierto de los Leones and the ecological park at Xochimilco. El Desierto de los Leones is an area where it is possible to see rare wildlife such as coyotes, rabbits and deer in the cool pine and oak forests. Xochimilco Ecological Park (see p. 45) is a wetland that is an important stopover for migratory birds. Unfortunately, the demands for land for housing means that even parts of protected areas are being built on. Around five km sq of forest is lost from Mexico City each year.

Another major government initiative involves reducing air pollution. In order to do this the government has been providing money to help convert vehicles to catalytic converters, to encourage the use of less polluting forms of fuel and to remove the oldest and most polluting vehicles from the city. This has been successful in the DF, but in the poorer parts of the city outside the DF the problem remains acute.

By far the most famous attempt to reduce pollution was the introduction of 'no-drive days'. Since 1989 the government has tried to limit the numbers of cars on the city's roads by banning each car from the roads for a given day each week. Although this worked initially it eventually led to many people buying an extra car just to be able to drive when their main car was off the road on the seventh day of the week.

▲ The city's parks, like Desierto de Los Leones, are a sanctuary for people in the enormous city.

It is estimated that around 34 per cent of all waste heading for the landfill sites is potentially recyclable. One famous campaign was started by the Junior League of Mexico in 1995. In the following 10 years they collected and recycled more than 25 million juice and milk cartons. Their 'Recyclable by Nature' programme was so successful at getting people to recycle cartons that, in 2004, the city government adopted it as the basis of a new law designed to encourage household waste to be separated for recycling.

▶ Plastic bottles ready for recycling.

▼ This is the site of an old landfill, now converted to a park and children's playground.

The Mexico City of tomorrow

In 1950 the Mexico City Metropolitan Area had fewer than three million inhabitants. Today it is more than six times larger. This extraordinary growth in population has inevitably put a massive strain on the city and national governments. Large numbers of jobs need to be created every year to provide employment for the tens of thousands of people who migrate to the city, and for young people finishing school and university. The demand for basic services such as clean water, electricity and hospitals increases every year. Mexico City also faces a very serious problem from air and water pollution.

Economic potential

The economic potential of Mexico and Mexico City is enormous. The country is rich in natural resources and has a relatively young and energetic population. This is particularly true when compared to its neighbour the USA, which has an ageing population and a shrinking workforce. Mexico and Mexico City's economies also benefit from their proximity to the USA and its huge consumer market. However, by the same token, Mexico City's economy is now so heavily dependent on the USA that any downturn in the USA economy has an almost immediate knock-on effect in Mexico City, as demand for goods falls and tourist numbers decline.

▼ The central business areas of Mexico City are as affluent as any in the world.

▲ Despite the wealth of the central DF, poverty stricken regions surround it.

The future

The election of a city mayor has allowed many of Mexico City's most pressing problems to be addressed directly for the first time. The first elected mayor, Andres Manuel Lopez Obrador, started many programmes, continued by his successors, to improve the living standards of the city's residents. Obrador stepped down as mayor in 2005 in order to stand for election as national president. A popular but controversial mayor, in 2000 he came second in a poll to determine the best city mayor in the world. His policies earned him praise and notoriety in equal measure.

To bring down the very high crime rate the Mayor brought Rudolph Giuliani, the ex-Mayor of New York to Mexico City, to put into practice the highly-successful zero tolerance approach to crime that he used in New York City.

In one imaginative move, the city government switched city computers from Microsoft to free Linux operating systems, with the money saved going to help the economically disadvantaged.

New housing is being built where it is most needed, and not where developers, hoping to make as large a profit as possible, would like to have it. In one powerful demonstration of the city government's intention to make changes, the lost parts of Chapultepec Park were reclaimed. Over the years the wealthy and powerful had moved into homes surrounding the park, and then, quite simply, taken some of it. The government ripped down the walls that had been built. 'No special interest groups,' said Obrador at the time, 'have any claim on us. We lick no one's boots. Deliver to the people – that's all we have to do.'

Glossary

Aquifer A layer of underground rock that soaks up and stores water.

Arid A term used to describe an environment with an annual rainfall of less that 250-300 mm.

Biodiversity The variation (diversity) of biological life in an area.

Chinampas An Aztec word for describing the floating gardens they used to grow crops in the swampy margins of Lake Texcoco.

Colonial A term used to describe a system where one country is occupied and ruled by a foreign country.

Delegaciones The name for one of the 16 areas that the Distrito Federal is divided into.

Deforestation The clearance of trees either for timber or for land.

Endemic A disease, or a plant, found only in a restricted location.

Erosion The removal of soil and rock by natural forces (wind and rain) or people (for example by deforestation - see entry above).

Fault line A line of weakness in the Earth's crust.

GDP (Gross Domestic Product) The monetary value of goods and services produced by a country in a single year.

Great Depression A period in the 1930s when the world economy went into a major recession caused by the collapse of the Stock Market on Wall Street in the USA.

Habitat The natural home of a living thing.

Informal economy The part of a nation's economy that is not recorded officially and for which no taxes are paid.

Infrastructure The basic economic foundations of the country such as roads, bridges, communication networks and proper sewerage systems.

Landfill A method of disposing of garbage by burying underground.

Life expectancy The number of years a person is expected to live.

Megacity A city with a population of over 10 million.

Mestizo A Spanish word describing people of mixed Indian and European race.

Migration To move from one area or country to settle in another, for example in search of work or better living conditions

Municipal Relating to a town, city or other region that has its own system of local government.

Municipios The name given to local areas in the state of Mexico.

Plateau (plural plateaux) A high flat area of land.

Production The part of a nation's economy where products are manufactured, mined or cultivated.

SARS A highly contagious disease properly known as Severe Acute Respiratory Syndrome (SARS) that emerged in Asia in 2002 and spread quickly as people travelled around the world.

Services Economic activities that are paid for although nothing is produced, such as tourism and banking.

Smog A combination of the words "smoke" and "fog" describing the mixture of pollutants in the air.

Sustainability Living in a way that does not spoil the world for future generations.

Temperate A climate characterised by mild temperatures.

Temperature inversion A phenomenon where cold air in the winter traps exhaust gases, preventing them from dispersing.

Terrestrial Land based.

Urbanisation The process by which a country's population becomes concentrated into towns and cities.

Further information

Useful websites

CIA World Factbook
www.cia.gov/cia/publications/factbook/
Facts and figures on every country in the world.

The Economist
www.economist.com/cities/
Information on some of the world's major cities, including Mexico City.

www.un.org/cyberschoolbus
A United Nations site aimed at school students with data on UN member countries.

Institute Nacional de Estadistica Geograpfiae y Informatica (INEGI) (National Institute of Statistics, Geography and Informatics)
www.inegi.gob.mx
A Spanish language website with some English documents available

United Nations Development Programme (UNDP)
www.undp.org
Information on UN development programmes.

United Nations Children Fund (UNICEF)
www.unicef.org
Information on the UN's work for children, with data from every member country.

World Wildlife Fund
www.panda.org/
Use the search engine to find details on wildlife conservation work in Mexico City.

Books

Non-fiction

Mexico City John Noble et al (Lonely Planet Publications, 2000)

Pocket Mexico City (Fodor Travel Publications Inc, 1998)

Mexico City Nick Caistor (C. Hurst and Co Publishers, 2000)

Mexico City Handbook Cummings et al (Avalon Travel Publishing, 2002)

Countries of the World Mexico Edward Parker (Evans, 2004)
Illustrated reference for KS2-3

The Changing face of Mexico Edward Parker (Hodder Wayland, 2001)
Reference for KS2-3

Nations of the World: Mexico Jen Green (Raintree, 2003)
Illustrated reference for in-depth study, with links to KS3-4.

Lonely Planet Guide: Mexico John Noble (Lonely Planet Publications, 2002) Budget travel guide for travellers of all ages.

Rough Guides: Mexico John Fisher (Rough Guides, 2001) Budget travel guide for travellers of all ages.

Fiction

Under the Volcano by Malcolm Lowry (Lippincot, 1965)
A story set in Mexico on the Day of the Dead in the late 1930s.

Index